Start Growing

'A flower blossoms
for its own joy'

OSCAR WILDE

Start Growing

A year of joyful gardening for absolute beginners

Daisy Payne

<u>Spring</u>

Summer

Autumn

Winter

Becoming
a gardener

In a world where we spend much of our time joined at the fingertips to our phones, I've found gardening to be the magic ingredient for helping me find inner peace, practise mindfulness or, as I prefer to think of it, simply feel a little joy in my day-to-day life. Connecting with the soil, enjoying the simple pleasure of growing something from seed, adding colour to your space with plants, breathing in the fresh air as you chop back a rose or clean up a patio – it's more satisfying than likes on Instagram, that's for sure.

My journey into gardening started when I bought my first home. It was a new build, so the garden was halfway between a mud patch and a building site when I first moved in. There was something quite exciting about having a totally blank canvas to work with but, never having done any gardening before, it also felt overwhelming. Where to start? The garden sloped down towards the side gate, with a shed at the top and a lot of fencing (as is usual with new builds). So how would it be possible to maximise the space on a budget and make it feel

like a place that I wanted to spend time in? How could I make it beautiful? Would anything ever grow? Fast-forward five years or so and my journey has been about not only learning the basics of gardening, but also finding the truest form of happiness through it. When I first drew out the design for my garden, little did I know that the best thing about the process wouldn't be the end result, but what I learnt along the way.

I made a lot of mistakes when I first started out, and I continue to do so. If I was creating that garden again, I'd probably do it completely differently! But that's the joy of gardening. You learn and you grow, just as your plants and the garden you're creating does. When I started, I struggled to get to grips with some of the practicalities of gardening, like how much things would cost, how long they'd take and, frankly, just how on earth to actually do it. So, whether you have ten minutes to spare between meetings while you work from home or a whole weekend free, I hope this book can guide you through your first steps into gardening and help you find the joy in it like I have. Remember, part of this will involve getting things wrong, not feeling like you've got it all completely figured out and holding onto that little bit of blind hope that it'll turn out how you want it to!

Over the following pages, I'll outline everything you need to know to get started. Then, we'll grow through the seasons together, with 40 fuss-free and easy-to-understand projects. If you have a big garden or not much space at all (perhaps even just a window ledge) and whatever your budget, there will be projects to excite you, help you unwind, give you some much needed headspace, get you outside and get your body moving. Whatever the time of year, there's gardening and growing for you to enjoy.

What you need
to get started

Taking that first step into gardening can be daunting, but you don't need to buy lots of equipment or spend lots of money. The reality is, you can do a lot with not a lot!

The tools you need to get started depend on the space you have. If you have a balcony garden that is likely to consist mostly of pots, for example, then you might not need any tools at all. All you need to plant up in pots is a good peat-free compost and the willingness to get your hands dirty.

If you have a slightly bigger space, you'll likely find a spade, fork, trowel and an edger helpful. An edger is a long-handled tool with a small, half-moon-shaped end, which is used to stop grass from straying onto the areas surrounding your lawn such as patios and paths. A watering can is useful, too, but not essential when you first start – you can always use other jugs or beakers to hold water while you get to grips with things.

Later down the line, or if you're taking care of an already established garden, you may want to get a kneeler. These pads or small cushioned benches are useful for saving your jeans

from getting too muddy and your knees from getting sore. If you're weeding, sowing or planting bulbs, a kneeler is a great thing to have in your garden toolkit.

I found a lot of my tools second-hand via social media listings and local groups – sites like these are great for picking up low-cost and free items, making getting into gardening that little bit easier.

Most of all, you need to be ready to get stuck in, learn and enjoy the fresh air and peacefulness that gardening can offer. Leave your phone inside and get outside!

Getting to grips with your garden

Windowsill? Balcony? Courtyard? Small lawn? Overgrown mess? Allotment? Getting to grips with your outside space, whatever it's like, is not something you should rush. It can be tempting to jump straight in and buy whatever is in bloom at the garden centre, but taking time to assess your space properly and make a plan so that you can nurture the perfect selection of plants is a vital part of building a brilliantly beautiful garden.

If you're overhauling a garden that already has a lot of plants in it, you should first assess what's there – what's good, bad and ugly? Don't rush into digging plants out or changing things too fast, as you might regret it later down the line. However, do look out for invasive weeds such as bindweed, knotweed and horsetail. If your garden has weeds that are taking over, you'll want to find ways to get rid of these so that you can nurture the plants you choose yourself. While generally I find it beneficial to keep my phone indoors when I'm gardening so I can take a break from it, plant identification apps can be a really helpful tool if you're not sure what's a weed and what isn't.

Identifying and removing weeds is a great place to start when beginning to plan your garden, but there are a few other key questions you should take into consideration:

— Where does the sun come into your garden and at what time in the day?
— How much shade is there in your garden or outside space and where is it?
— What do you already like about the space, and if there are plants already established, are they healthy or do they look a bit dishevelled?
— How much time do you have on a daily or weekly basis to spend in your garden?

Once you've understood the basics of your garden and got a feel for how it works, you'll be ready to start thinking about your plans for the space and how you'd like to use it.

Figuring out your garden plan

Garden planning doesn't need to be complicated. My ethos is simple – create a space that you want to spend time in and that suits your life and your needs.

First, write a list of the things you want to be able to do in your garden – that might be relaxing, socialising, playing with your dog or entertaining the kids. Be realistic about the practical uses your garden will need to have and how much it can do. The same applies to balcony gardens – when you're limited on space, you can get creative with how you design it, but it's key that you decide what your priority is for the space. For example, if you love cooking and entertaining, then incorporating herbs to use in recipes and cocktails might be something to prioritise. Or, if you'd like to use your space to relax, then planting rosemary and camomile might be worthwhile, as they are beautiful and have relaxing properties, too!

Once you've put together your wish list, you can start to consider the style of garden you'd like to create and then the planting scheme, budget and timescales. Take your time and don't feel the need to get every single aspect of your garden 'done' straight away. Developing your garden over time is the best way, and this helps to keep costs down, too.

As you start to consider what you want out of your garden, it's important to spend some time sussing out where and when the sun comes in. This will vary over the year, so you may want to take your time on this. Knowing where your sunny spots and shady spots are all year round will help you plan out the types of plants that will likely thrive in your garden. Never skip checking a plant's label before you buy it to make sure it'll be suited to where you want to put it.

When it comes to deciding on a planting scheme, I start by thinking about the colours and there's no better way to get inspiration than by visiting your nearest open gardens, garden centre or having a flick through a magazine. Consider height too, and how much space you have to work with. Always plant up any border (see page 30) with gaps between plants to start with – less is often more – you'll thank yourself for it in years to come! When it comes to selecting plants, start by testing your soil (see page 18) and go from there!

Budgeting is crucial too. It can be tempting to go plant shopping and end up buying everything that's in flower there and then, inevitably wasting money and not getting around to planting everything (guilty!). Instead, I like to research plants before I go shopping, so I have a clear list and know what I want to buy, for where. Buying plants with purpose is the best way to keep the cost down. Look beyond garden centres too (although they are wonderful, and I love my local garden centres deeply!). Try visiting nurseries – and always ask questions – the plant people are incredibly knowledgeable and are there to help you. This book will help you too!

Garden styles

No matter what size your garden (and, in my opinion, pots by the front door or a window box count), there are many different gardening styles that you can draw inspiration from when planning your own space. Spending time online looking at the different types of gardens that are out there can really help, but it can be hard to translate that into a straightforward shopping list for the garden centre. Below I've listed some of the main garden styles and how best to achieve them at home.

Contemporary

If you like clean lines, light colours and an orderly feel in your spaces, then a contemporary style can be achieved with structure, bold shapes and minimalist planting. Consider sleek materials and square pots.

Mediterranean

If you'd like to create a Mediterranean style for your garden, the best way to do that is by using terracotta pots. You can also consider using gravel as a topper around your plants and in dining spaces, incorporating water features and including drought-tolerant plants or succulents in your plan.

Formal

Formal gardens have a clear structure and are usually symmetrical in layout. The key for this kind of garden is balance and a careful and detailed plan, to make sure that there's symmetry in the planting.

Urban

Urban gardens tend to be surrounded by high walls and other buildings and can often be shady, although that's not always the case. If you're planning an urban garden, you'll need to make every centimetre count, and you may need to consider using compact plants that don't take up much space. You may also need to be smart with what furniture you choose. Consider how you can use the height around you to incorporate plants creatively, too.

Cottage and wildlife friendly

Cottage gardens are generally a little more wild and meandering, with deep borders and a multitude of plants. This is the total opposite of the contemporary or formal garden. When creating a garden like this, consider how you use paths and walkways to draw the eye, and go deep with your planting.

Allotment

If you have an allotment or would like to create a space for growing your own veg, the key is to make sure you can access everything you grow. This means you can keep a close eye on your plants and also allows for easier maintenance. It makes sense to grow in rows for this reason, as well as to make it easier to spot weeds. It's also important to mix up what you plant every year, so that the soil is the healthiest it can be.

Upcycled

This is one of my favourite styles to embrace in the garden – it's all about repurposing and recycling objects so that they take on a new life. This can help bring amazing character to your garden and can keep costs down, too. Pallets are great for repurposing into planters, shelves can be used to house plants, and old buckets and sinks make great pots.

Testing your soil: what's its type and why does it matter?

We all have a type – and no, I'm not talking about our love lives here! Did you know that not all soil is the same? There are different types of soil, which means that different types of plants thrive in some locations and not in others. This is all down to the level of acidity in the soil. Do you remember the science lesson at school about the pH scale? That's what this is all about.

Before finalising your garden plan or planting anything, the first job is to test the soil so you know what soil type you are working with. This can be done with a home testing kit, which you can buy from a garden centre. Once you've determined the acidity of your soil, consider the types of plants and flowers that you'd like to enjoy in your outside space and which are suited to your soil type.

What grows well in alkaline soil?

— Hydrangeas
— Sweet peas
— Foxgloves
— Clematis
— Honeysuckle
— Geraniums
— Beetroot
— Cauliflower
— Cabbages

What grows well in acid soil?

— Maples
— Azaleas
— Rhododendrons
— Camellias
— Viburnum
— Magnolias

When potting on seedlings (see pages 33, 45 and 181), try to avoid using soil from your garden. It's best to get your hands on a bag of peat-free compost if you can. This is because the soil in your garden won't hold as much water as a good compost will, and your young plants will need it to grow.

Why peat-free?

Peat is a natural material made from an accumulation of partially decayed vegetation or organic matter and is created by sphagnum mosses growing in bogs. It acts as a carbon sink, absorbing large amounts of carbon dioxide from its surrounding environment.

Peat is harvested for use in compost and for burning in electricity generation. To harvest it, the bogs are drained and cleared of all vegetation. Harvesting not only removes a layer of peat of around 20cm every year – in other words, a century's worth of peat accumulation – but releases the carbon dioxide that had been stored within it.

As well as storing carbon dioxide, peat bogs are also invaluable habitats for wildlife and natural flood defences, soaking up excess rainfall and releasing it slowly. The extraction of peat wipes out the entire ecosystem.

It's therefore imperative to preserve peat for the good of the environment. Compost manufacturers have missed successive deadlines for the end of peat compost, but they are now under increasing pressure to reduce the percentage of peat in their products, and, ideally, to replace them with peat-free products. Peat-free composts are typically made from materials such as wood fibre, composted bark and coir (coconut fibre) – the latter is what I'm using below. The more we all buy peat-free, the more demand there is for more environmentally friendly composts. Home composting is also a brilliant way of doing your bit for the environment (see page 111).

To dig or not to dig?

That is the question... Your instinct may be to get digging in your garden straight away, but did you know that there is also a no-dig method you could try? Pioneered by English horticulturalist Charles Dowding, the method is very simple and might be particularly well suited to you if you're not in a rush to jazz up your garden, you have few weeds, you're thinking of creating raised beds or if you'd like to grow fruit and vegetables.

To follow the no-dig method, you layer up cardboard wherever you'd like to plant up in the future, dampen it with water using a watering can or hose and add a very thick mulch of compost. After several weeks, your no dig beds will be ready to use.

Of course, this method won't be the most suitable for every application – and digging can be one of the most enjoyable parts of gardening! In some areas in my garden I have utilised the no-dig method and in others I've got stuck into the soil with my spade and fork. I have recently had to get rid of some really invasive weeds, and I've found that digging in and removing the root has been the best option for me. Consider how much time you have and your garden style, and then you can decide whether you want to dig or not.

Dig ...

No dig ...

Keeping slugs and pests away

An important part of getting to grips with gardening is knowing how to keep your plants healthy and free from pests in a natural way. I believe that a natural approach is best as it does not damage the biodiversity of your outside space.

Sap-sucking aphids, also known as greenfly or blackfly, are the most common garden pest. They are tiny – blink and you'll miss them. I've found that they love roses and young plants the best. Checking on your plants every couple of days and flicking off the aphids is the best natural way to get rid of them.

If you plant something one day and then go back to it the next and find that its leaves have all been nibbled, then you're most likely dealing with slugs. They are one of the most common pests you'll come across in the garden. Nothing is safe from slugs – they can even find their way into pots. The best solution I've found is to protect your plants by placing a ring of wool pellets around the stems on the soil surface, which you can buy online or in garden centres. Grit also works well as an alternative. The slugs don't like the texture of them and won't go near your plants. This is particularly effective for young plants.

If you live in a more urban environment, you may find that pigeons, foxes and squirrels are common in your garden. Foxes and squirrels may dig up newly planted plants, and you can try using the scent of things they hate to deter them. These animals dislike garlic and chilli, so try spraying your plants with an infused water in a spray bottle. These deterrents probably won't stick around for too long, though, so you might want to consider more plants in pots to help navigate this.

When it comes to pigeons, you may have seen the occasional CD hanging up in an allotment and wondered why it was there. It's because pigeons are put off by shiny things, so hanging CDs is one way of keeping them away from your garden or allotment.

While not a living thing, frost is the final key pest to consider. In winter, keep an eye on the weather forecast, and if temperatures are likely to drop below freezing, then it's

vital you take care of your plants, particularly those that are still flowering in the winter months. Keep them cosy with some fleecing (you can buy this from your local garden centre or online) or reuse blankets or clothing. Just be sure to give them some light during the day or as temperatures warm up.

Spr

ing

Creating a border

Creating structure by forming planting areas in your garden is the perfect first step in your gardening journey, and spring is the time to get started. Borders typically separate different garden features like lawns, beds and pathways, and they are great if you want to add colour, height or interest.

WHAT YOU NEED

String, canes or hose pipe
A garden fork
An edger
A plank of wood

A spade
Peat-free multipurpose
  compost (you may need
  a couple of bags)

HOW LONG YOU NEED
The time you will need depends on the size of the border you're creating. For a small border area, you may need only 30 minutes or so, but for larger spaces, you may need to set aside up to a day.

The joy it brings...

—

Creating borders is a very satisfying gardening task and it often signals the start of a new chapter in your outside space. For me, there's nothing more joyful than knowing I'm preparing space for plants to thrive.

1. Decide on the size and shape of border you want to create – if you're not sure, keep it simple. Mock up the area where you want the border to be, using canes and twine (or even your hose) to create an outline.

2. Prepare the ground, removing any existing plants or weeds. Loosen the soil by pricking it with a garden fork and remove any grass with a spade.

3. For a smart edge, follow the line you have laid our with an edger, cleanly slicing the grass in a downward motion.

4. Finally, mulch your border (see page 129) with the compost.

Sowing pretty cosmos

WHY YOU SHOULD GIVE IT A TRY
Cosmos are easy to grow from seed, so if you've never tried this before they are a good plant to start with. They are very pretty flowers and look stunning in borders or in pots.

WHAT YOU NEED
Cosmos seeds
Small pots (up
to 10cm diameter)

Peat-free seed compost
A sunny windowsill

HOW LONG YOU NEED
As long as you'd like! You can plant up these easy seeds in five minutes or spend an hour enjoying the task.

The joy it brings...

—

Cosmos are delicate flowers that accentuate any size or style of garden. When you look outside, you'll be full of pride knowing you've grown them yourself from seed.

1. Fill the pots three-quarters full with seed compost and use a pen or pencil to create a shallow hole to sow the seed. In a pot this size, you can add up to three seeds, evenly spaced.

2. Drop a seed into each hole, cover with more compost and then firm down with your hand.

3. Remember what you've planted by re-using an old lolly stick to label your pots and then place in a sunny spot.

4. Water immediately, then every couple of days and soon you'll see the germinated seedlings. Leave indoors for a few weeks, then plant outside in warmer weather.

Planting roses

WHY YOU SHOULD GIVE IT A TRY

Every garden is made brighter with a rose. The great thing about roses is that they come in so many different sizes, shapes and colours, so there really is a rose for every garden. Roses can be planted in pots or in borders.

WHAT YOU NEED

A bare-root or potted rose plant

Peat-free multipurpose compost

HOW LONG YOU NEED

15–30 minutes.

The joy it brings...

—

Roses are one of my favourite flowers. There are many varieties, with different perfumes as well as colours and sizes. They're romantic and will make any garden feel special.

1. Dig a hole that's double the size of the pot the rose is in or, if you're planting a bare-root plant, a hole that is deep enough to hold the roots of the rose.

2. Throw a few handfuls of compost into the hole, then place the rose in and fill with more compost.

3. Firm down around the rose with your hands. You can also firm it down further by gently pressing around the base of the plant with your feet.

4. Water well, then sit back and watch your rose bloom come the summer!

A colourful spring display

WHY YOU SHOULD GIVE IT A TRY

Not only does bringing spring colours into your garden, balcony or patio fill it with happiness, but spending time outside as the weather warms up gives you the chance to soak in some much-needed vitamin D from the sun. Bedding plants are fast-growing plants (usually annuals).

WHAT YOU NEED

Spring bedding plants
  such as violas, primroses
  and daffodils

Pots
Peat-free multipurpose
  compost

HOW LONG YOU NEED

A couple of pots can be planted up quickly, but spend a whole afternoon doing this if you fancy it!

The joy it brings...

—

Listening out for birdsong while you're outside planting spring displays is a calming, mindful activity.

1. Half-fill the pots with compost and select the plants for each pot – I like to contrast colours to create an impact.

2. Place the plants into the pots so that they sit just below the top of the pot – you should be able to fit three or four plants in a medium-sized pot.

3. Fill around the plants with more compost, then gently push it down with your fingertips.

4. Water the plants and place them in a sunny, sheltered spot. If there's no rain for a week or so, water them again so that they keep thriving.

Growing your own strawberries

WHY YOU SHOULD GIVE IT A TRY

Growing your own strawberries is great fun and it's a perfect first crop if you've never grown anything before. Strawberries grow well in containers – in fact, they're best grown in them. And there's nothing sweeter than a sun-ripened strawberry in late spring and summer!

WHAT YOU NEED

Potted strawberry plants
A container of your choice – either a pot, a window box or a hanging basket
Peat-free multipurpose compost
Tomato feed

HOW LONG YOU NEED

You can plant these out in less than 30 minutes.

The joy it brings...

—

Nipping outside in your dressing gown and slippers in the morning to pick your own strawberries to go with your porridge is an amazing feeling – I would definitely recommend.

1. Half-fill the container with compost.

2. Loosen the strawberry plants from their pots and place in the container, spacing them about 10cm apart.

3. Fill the container with more compost around the plants, firm down the soil with your hands, and then place in a sunny spot.

4. Water well and use a tomato feed when the plants start fruiting, as this will make your strawberries even more delicious and juicy! Pick and eat when the strawberries have turned red.

The tomato project

WHY YOU SHOULD GIVE IT A TRY

Growing your own tomatoes is not only great fun, but you'll also be rewarded with truly delicious, juicy fruits that you can eat fresh or cook with every day. Tomatoes are easy to grow and can be sown indoors from March and then moved outside later in spring once the weather has warmed up. There are lots of varieties of tomato and different types of plants to choose from – if you have limited space, pick a bush variety as they're compact and won't take up too much of your space.

WHAT YOU NEED

Tomato seeds (there are lots to choose from, so pick plants that are best suited to your space)

Peat-free seed and multipurpose compost

A small pot (up to 10cm diameter) for sowing and three larger outdoor pots for when the seedlings have developed

A sunny, warm windowsill

HOW LONG YOU NEED

You'll need a little time each week to tend to your plants, first as seedlings and then by watering and feeding your established plants. Every few days, water and check on them.

The joy it brings...

—

Tomatoes are one of my kitchen staples and knowing they've been grown in my own garden really feels good. And, with so many different varieties, you can pick a tomato that best suits you!

1. Fill the smaller pots with seed compost. Water gently then place a seed on top and cover thinly with more compost. Put the pot on a sunny windowsill and water every couple of days.

2. Once your little tomato plant has started to grow, it's time to 'pot on' into individual pots. To do this, lightly squeeze the pot it's growing in to loosen the soil and gently pull the tomato seedling out.

3. Repot your seedling into a larger pot and water well. You might want to repot a few times as it grows larger, moving to a bigger pot every time.

4. In warmer weather, once your plant has established, it will flower, then fruit! Once tomatoes develop, keep well watered, using tomato or seaweed feed every week or two. If it needs support, see page 48.

Setting up plant supports

WHY YOU SHOULD GIVE IT A TRY

Many tall plants will need support through the spring and summer to help them grow upright and stay healthy. Placing supports in the right place early in the year means your plants will benefit straight away. There are lots of different types of plant supports, such as canes, stakes, cages and trellises. The type of plant support you choose will depend on the type of plant you're growing and its growth habit. For example, tall, vining plants like tomatoes may require a sturdy stake or trellis.

WHAT YOU NEED

Canes or plant supports

Twine or string

HOW LONG YOU NEED

Just a few minutes.

The joy it brings...

—

Later in the season, you'll be glad you took the time to give your plants the support they need. They will look and grow better, and if there is a spell of heavy rain, your plants will be more likely to bounce back afterwards.

Setting up supports when your plants are newly planted is always best. If you're using stakes or canes, push them into the ground near the plant, being careful not to damage the roots.

A conical support is good for plants with floppy or heavy flowers such as peonies and hydrangeas. Add them in as early as you can, before they flower.

Trellis is fantastic for climbing plants and is easy to install. Train your plants up the supports by tying them in too (see page 72).

Chitting and growing potatoes

WHY YOU SHOULD GIVE IT A TRY

First of all, it's incredibly easy, but if that isn't persuasion enough, how about the satisfaction of cooking up homegrown potatoes for your family or friends, knowing exactly where they came from? Chitting (sprouting seed potatoes before planting) is easy and potato plants also take up very little space, so if you have a courtyard garden, this is a grow-your-own option for you! My favourite variety of potato to grow is Charlotte – they're delicious when roasted!

WHAT YOU NEED

Seed potatoes (it's important to buy seed potatoes because they're free of any nasties and will give you the best possible crop – you can find them online or at garden centres)

Egg cartons or a tray
Something to grow your potatoes in – if you don't have a veg patch or raised bed, try a large pot or a potato grow bag
Peat-free multipurpose compost

HOW LONG YOU NEED

Chitting your potatoes will take about five minutes to set up and then a further two weeks to sprout. The potatoes then take about 80 days to grow.

The joy it brings...

—

The taste of your first homegrown potato is one you'll never forget.

1. Place a seed potato in each hole of an egg carton or place on a tray, then transfer to a cool, light spot (near a windowsill is perfect) to chit.

2. Once they are sprouting big green shoots, prepare a container for growing. Make sure it has several holes in the bottom for drainage, then fill it one-third full with compost.

3. Plant the potatoes a hand's distance apart, with the sprouts facing upwards. Cover with compost until the container is half full, then water well. Leave in a warm sunny place.

4. As the potatoes grow, keep adding compost to the container to bury the stems. In late summer when the foliage turns yellow, your crop is ready! Empty the pot, clean off the compost and enjoy.

Growing dahlias

WHY YOU SHOULD GIVE IT A TRY

Dahlias are grown from tubers, which makes them rather different to your usual flower! Tubers look like something that might have escaped from a Hogwarts herbology class – they are a type of plant food storage vessel that grow in clusters and they come in a range of sizes. When growing dahlias, I like to pick different types and heights to create a varied display. They make great cut flowers, too, so they can bring colour inside your home as well as to your outside space. Be sure to put your dahlias in a sunny spot – you'll be rewarded with beautiful blooms in late summer.

WHAT YOU NEED

A packet of dahlia tubers (available in garden centres from February/March)

Peat-free multipurpose compost

A 30cm diameter pot or a border that gets plenty of sunshine

HOW LONG YOU NEED

It takes less than 30 minutes to plant three tubers.

The joy it brings...

—

Planting a tuber underground feels a little mysterious – and when the dahlia flowers bloom, it's dazzling! You'll get many flowers from your tubers and they make a wonderful late summer display.

1. Fill the pot with compost to around three-quarters full. Put the dahlia tuber in the soil with the old stem at the top and the little stringy bits at the bottom.

2. Fill the rest of the pot with compost, making sure it's firmed down and the top of the tuber is just poking out of the top. Water well and place in a sunny spot, then continue to water regularly.

3. Within a few weeks you'll see the start of new life. Continue to water regularly.

4. Provide support to the plant if needed (see page 48). In autumn, dig up the tubers (see page 120) and store them in a frost-free spot until next spring.

Sweet pea heaven

WHY YOU SHOULD GIVE IT A TRY
Growing sweet peas is fun and easy! They're fragrant, colourful, don't need loads of space to thrive and they give you an abundance of flowers throughout spring and summer. Picking them creates even more flowers and sweet peas look so pretty in a small vase on a table or windowsill.

WHAT YOU NEED
Sweet pea seeds
Small pots
Peat-free seed compost
Plant supports (when you get to summer)

HOW LONG YOU NEED
Around 15 minutes to sow (after a couple of hours' soaking), then a little time every couple of days to check in on your seedlings. When it comes to planting them out, you'll need no more than 15 minutes.

The joy it brings...

—

Sweet peas were one of the first
flowers I ever grew from seed.
They smell amazing and the flowers
are intricate and beautiful.

1. Soak the sweet pea seeds in a glass or small container of water for a few hours.

2. Fill the pots with seed compost and sow two seeds per pot, poking them about 2cm deep into the soil.

3. When the plants are about 15cm tall, they're ready to get used to the outdoors. Put them in a sheltered spot but don't plant them just yet.

4. After the last frost, plant your sweet peas. They're climbers, so need something like a trellis, canes or an obelisk. Water well and pick the flowers lots in summer so more grow

SPRING

Sum

mer

When and how to water your plants

WHY YOU SHOULD GIVE IT A TRY

Water is essential for the survival of your plants. It is a crucial component in photosynthesis, which is the process by which plants produce the energy they need to grow. Watering your plants regularly can also help to prevent pests and diseases. A well-hydrated plant is less susceptible to attack as it is better able to defend itself. A tip from me: overwatering is one of the most common mistakes that beginner gardeners make. Too much water can lead to root rot, fungal diseases and even the death of the plant. Always try to avoid watering until the soil has dried out a bit.

WHAT YOU NEED

A watering can, jug or hose   Water – either collected as rainwater or from your tap

HOW LONG YOU NEED

The time you need to spend watering your plants will depend on the weather (if it's been hot and whether or not it has rained), the type of plants you have, your soil type and the size of your pots or garden borders. I recommend checking your plants every day if you can (see step 1 opposite).

The joy it brings...

—

Watering infrequently but deeply is good for your plants and I find it really relaxing and fulfilling.

1. Before you do any watering, check the soil moisture level by sticking your finger about an inch into the soil. If it feels dry to the touch, it's time to water. If the soil is still moist, wait a day or two and check again.

2. Either early in the morning or in the evening, when the temperature is cooler, fill up your watering can or get your hose ready.

3. Focus your watering at the base of the plant. Water deeply so that the water reaches the root zone. This encourages deep root growth and helps the plant to withstand drought conditions.

4. Mulch around your plants regularly (see page 129). This aids water retention, so it'll mean your plants are healthier!

Keeping on top of weeds the easy way

WHY YOU SHOULD GIVE IT A TRY

The goal of every gardener is to have healthy plants. Getting rid of weeds without using chemicals will give your plants more space to thrive without competing with other plants. Troublesome weeds (plants that are wild and in the wrong place) are your enemy, as they may strangle or kill your healthy plants – the key is to remove these weeds from the root as quickly as you can when you first spot them.

WHAT YOU NEED

A trowel   Gardening gloves

HOW LONG YOU NEED

30 minutes or a little time every day

The joy it brings...

—

I find weeding very satisfying as a gardening job, and ultimately it means you will have happy plants that can thrive in their environment. Keeping an eye on your outside space is vital to keeping it healthy and therefore an enjoyable place to spend time in.

1. Take a look around your garden or into your pots and locate where you have weeds growing.

2. Wearing gloves, push your trowel into the soil around a weed.

3. Grip the weed at its base and gently pull upwards, taking care to remove the entire root system if you can.

4. Dispose of the weed in your garden waste – do not add it to your compost heap, as it may seed and end up in your garden again.

Tying in your plants

WHY YOU SHOULD GIVE IT A TRY
Tying in refers to the act of supporting tall plants and climbers as they grow, and it is an important part of maintaining your garden in summer. Keep an eye on your plants throughout the season, tying in and securing them when needed, particularly ahead of any heavy summer rainfall.

WHAT YOU NEED
Plant ties or gardening twine   Scissors

HOW LONG YOU NEED
10–15 minutes.

The joy it brings...

—

Who doesn't want to bring
a little extra pizazz to the garden over
summer? There's nothing worse than
seeing a lovely garden let down by
droopy flowers or a lack of maintenance,
so keep on top of your garden and
the needs of your plants to take
your outside space
to the next level.

1. Gently move the plant into the desired position or direction, taking care not to break or damage it.

2. Use soft plant ties or twine to secure the plant to the support structure. If you're using twine, like I am here, be sure to cut plenty to use.

3. Make sure it's not too tight so that the plant has room to move a little.

4. Once the plant has established itself, it might not require additional support or training, so remove the ties carefully so it can grow and maintain health.

Deadheading a rose

WHY YOU SHOULD GIVE IT A TRY
A rose that's healthy and in full bloom will always be one that has been efficiently deadheaded. This term refers to the removal of dead flowers to keep a plant looking its best and, depending on the type of rose, encourage new life. Different types of roses may have slightly different deadheading requirements, so be sure to check for specific instructions for the type of roses you are growing.

WHAT YOU NEED
Sharp, clean secateurs

A basket or bucket to collect the old blooms

HOW LONG YOU NEED
The time it takes will depend on the size of your rose and how established it is, but generally, a little time every week or so will do the trick.

The joy it brings...

—

Taking time every week to deadhead my roses gives me such joy – the fragrance of a rose is bliss and getting up close with the beauty of these flowers is a luxury.

1. Look for any faded, dry, dead flowers on your rose. These are the flowers that have finished blooming and are now ready to be removed carefully.

2. Chop the stem a few centimetres below the flower, and put the dead flower in your container, ready for the compost bin, if you have one.

3. Repeat until all the dead blooms have been removed. You may need to do this weekly throughout the summer months.

4. If your rose is a repeat-flowerer and you're watering regularly, you will be rewarded with fresh blooms throughout the summer.

Lifting bulbs to store for next year

WHY YOU SHOULD GIVE IT A TRY
When plants such as tulips die back in the summer, the bulbs can be lifted from the soil and stored, ready to plant again in autumn. It's really worth taking the time to do this if you are growing bulbs as it means that you can switch up your pots through the seasons and you can change where you plant the bulbs, too.

WHAT YOU NEED
A garden fork
Cardboard boxes or clean
  plastic plant pots

A cool, dark place to store
  the bulbs

HOW LONG YOU NEED
About 30 minutes.

The joy it brings...

—

Lifting bulbs means you can make way for new colour in your pots, making the most of your space in every season. It's a joyous thing knowing you have the plants safe to enjoy next year, while also enabling even more planting this season.

1. Tulip bulbs should be lifted and stored after the foliage has yellowed and died back naturally.

2. Carefully lift the bulbs using a fork or trowel. Be gentle so you don't damage the bulbs. If your tulips are in pots, simply loosen the soil and tip the pot upside down.

3. Remove the soil from around the bulbs and discard any bulbs that are soft or look a little mouldy.

4. Place the bulbs in a box or clean pot, label, and store in a cool, dry place. After a few days, when dry, remove the foliage, then leave over summer, ready to be replanted in autumn.

Making a water feature in a pot

WHY YOU SHOULD GIVE IT A TRY
If you're low on space, you might think a water feature would
be out of reach for you, but creating one in a pot is a brilliant way
to add an extra bit of interest to your outdoor area without taking
up too much valuable room.

WHAT YOU NEED
A large pot with no
    drainage holes
A smaller plastic pot that fits
    inside the larger pot
A solar-panelled water pump

A plant pot saucer with a
    hole made in the centre
    that fits over the top of
    the larger pot
Stones, to decorate

HOW LONG YOU NEED
1 hour.

The joy it brings...

—

The sound of running water is relaxing
and adds an extra dimension to your
garden or outdoor space – perfect for
while you enjoy the warm summer
months outdoors, perhaps sipping
a cocktail or sunbathing.

1. Put the small plastic pot inside the main pot, then place the water pump on top of it.

2. Make a hole in your plant pot saucer and place over the pump, sitting it on top.

3. Use the stones to decorate around the base of the pump.

4. Pour water into the top of your new water feature, set the pot in the sun and wait for the pump to start working.

Growing herbs on your windowsill

WHY YOU SHOULD GIVE IT A TRY

Take your cooking and hosting to the next level by creating your own fresh herb garden on a windowsill or in pots in your garden. When you're new to gardening, herbs are great to get started with because there are so many different types and they are fairly easy to grow. A top tip from me if you're growing mint: plant it on its own as it'll take over any other plants in the same pot.

WHAT YOU NEED

Peat-free multipurpose compost
Horticultural grit if you're planting Mediterranean herbs such as rosemary, chives and mint

Pots that will fit your chosen space – you can often buy small to medium-sized pots in sets with saucers that sit underneath
Herb plants of your choice

HOW LONG YOU NEED

15 minutes.

The joy it brings...

—

If you love cooking, you'll love the satisfaction that comes from growing your own herbs. They are easy to grow and look pretty in pots on your windowsill – you don't even need a garden!

1. Mix up the compost with a handful of grit and use it to half-fill each pot. Aim for three-quarters compost to a quarter grit.

2. Place a plant into each pot, or if planting multiple herbs, space them 10–15cm apart.

3. Add more of the compost mix and firm down around the plant with your fingers.

4. Water well, then let the water drain off. Position your pots on a sunny windowsill.

Growing herbs on your windowsill cont.

Summer hanging baskets

WHY YOU SHOULD GIVE IT A TRY

Filling hanging baskets with summer bedding plants is a relatively low-cost way of bringing colour into your garden or outdoor space – and you can never have too much colour during summer, in my opinion!

WHAT YOU NEED

Geranium plants – one or two per basket

Lobelia plants – these are a great 'filler', so you can add three or four per basket

Petunia plants – also a great filler, so add three or four per basket

Peat-free multipurpose compost

A hanging basket

A sponge (optional) - helps plant retain moisture

HOW LONG YOU NEED

30 minutes.

The joy it brings...

—

Colour in the garden is always a must for me and ensuring it right through the summer brings a joyful dimension to the garden.

1. Place the hanging basket in a pot so that it doesn't rock when planting up.

2. Half-fill the basket with compost, then cut up the sponge into four pieces and place it on top of the compost.

3. Surround the sponge with the bedding plants, making sure you put trailing plants (such as lobelia) around the side.

4. Top up with compost and firm down the soil with your fingers, then water well. Hang up and enjoy!

Planting veg

WHY YOU SHOULD GIVE IT A TRY

In the height of summer you're probably not going to be thinking about Christmas (unless you're a very organised present-buyer!), but in late July and early August there's still time to get growing in time for Christmas by fast-tracking your crop with the help of some young plants from your garden centre.

WHAT YOU NEED

Sprout plug plants
Carrot plug plants
Red cabbage plug plants

Peat-free multipurpose
 compost
Pots or trugs – or space in your
 raised beds or borders

HOW LONG YOU NEED

45 minutes.

The joy it brings...

—

The taste of homegrown vegetables is unrivalled – they are the freshest you can get, and the pride you'll feel at having grown them yourself is the best!

1. If you're planting in pots or trugs, fill them with compost. Otherwise, prepare the soil for planting by clearing any unwanted weeds and loosening the soil.

2. Measure out using the following spacing guidelines: for sprouts and cabbage, leave about 40–60cm between each plant, and for carrots, around 20–30cm.

3. Dig holes in the soil large enough for your plants, then place them into the holes, add more soil and firm down, then water.

4. Water every week or so and watch the plants grow, ready for cooking and eating in December.

Jazz up your patio for parties

WHY YOU SHOULD GIVE IT A TRY
Bring an unloved patio to life with plants, soft furnishings and colour. Far too often our patios are left dull and uninspiring, when they should be central to our summers.

WHAT YOU NEED
Potted plants, such as flowers, shrubs and small trees
Outdoor lighting

Decorative items, such as outdoor rugs, throw pillows or cushions
Screens, trellises or planters

HOW LONG YOU NEED
It totally depends on how much decorating you want to do – start small or go big!

The joy it brings...

—

I love entertaining and want to enjoy as much time as possible dining or relaxing in the garden. Don't be afraid of livening up your patio – it will make your summer days so much brighter.

1. Place your chosen potted plants around the patio in groups or standing alone, paying special attention to how you mix height and colour.

2. String up some lights or add stake lights or candles.

3. Create cosy seating areas, and add pops of colour with accessories, such as cushions, pillows and outdoor rugs.

4. Use screens, trellises or planters filled with tall plants to create privacy on your patio.

Aut

umn

Tidying your borders and pots

WHY YOU SHOULD GIVE IT A TRY
During autumn, it's a good idea to spend time getting your garden in good order before winter descends. I like to make sure that every plant in the garden looks tidy and healthy before the cold weather hits, so that by springtime they will be in the best shape they can be. As temperatures cool, use the time to have a really good tidy-up. Your future self will thank you for it!

WHAT YOU NEED
A bucket or big tub   Gardening gloves

HOW LONG YOU NEED
1 hour.

The joy it brings...

—

I love nothing more than a good sort-out in the garden. Making this an autumn ritual provides a good opportunity to take stock and check everything over.

1. Review your borders and pots and work out which plants are still going strong and what is dying back or looking a bit messy and needs chopping back now (see page 144).

2. If there's new life or a plant is still in bloom, leave it alone, and if there are seed heads on plants, leave these, too, as they are great for birds.

3. Collect up any fallen leaves and add to your compost heap, if you have one.

4. Remove any weeds to ensure your plants remain healthy over winter.

Cleaning your pots

WHY YOU SHOULD GIVE IT A TRY
Cleaning your pots is the ultimate in gardening job satisfaction and it's vital for next spring's growing as keeping things clean is important for the health of your plants.

WHAT YOU NEED
Washing-up liquid   A brush

HOW LONG YOU NEED
About 30 minutes, depending on how many pots you have.

The joy it brings...

—

Forget spring cleaning, getting outside in autumn when we are so often cooped up indoors and taking some time to ready the pots for next year is both invigorating and satisfying.

1. Empty out any pots containing plants that have died off (ideally into your compost heap).

2. Rinse the pots out with water, then give them a scrub with a brush and some soapy water.

3. Rinse again until all loose dirt is removed but don't worry about staining - this is normal and won't effect the health of your plants.

4. Let them air dry then plant bulbs in them ready for spring or store them somewhere dry.

Making your own bird feeder

WHY YOU SHOULD GIVE IT A TRY
Give the birds a tasty treat and entice them into your garden to increase its biodiversity! There are other benefits to welcoming birds into the garden, too, including improving your wellbeing and mental health. I love listening to them sing and watching them explore my outdoor space.

WHAT YOU NEED

A cardboard toilet roll
  or kitchen roll tube
Bird-friendly peanut butter
Spoon

A tray
Bird feed
Ribbon or string
A medium-sized stick

HOW LONG YOU NEED
15 minutes.

The joy it brings...

—

Watching different species of birds visit your garden is calming and connects you with nature. It really makes you realise how much life depends on our wonderful gardens. I find it very grounding, and you might just, too.

1. Poke or cut two holes in opposite sides at the top of the cardboard tube and two at the base.

2. Using a spoon, cover the tube in bird-friendly peanut butter.

3. Spread the bird feed out on a tray and roll the tube in the feed so that the whole of the roll is covered.

4. Thread the ribbon or string through the holes at the top of the roll and place the stick through the bottom two holes. Hang up your bird feeder and let the birds enjoy!

Home composting, whatever the size of your garden

WHY YOU SHOULD GIVE IT A TRY
Recycling compostable materials means you're sending less waste to landfill and by the end of the process, you will have created a healthy, homemade mulch for your garden or pots.

WHAT YOU NEED
A compost bin or, if you're short on space, a bokashi composter (a Japanese method of composting that pickles your kitchen waste)

HOW LONG YOU NEED
A little time and attention every day.

The joy it brings...

—

What better way to do your bit every day for your garden and, in turn, for the planet? Everyone should have a compost bin!

1. If you have a traditional compost bin, put any grass clippings, fallen leaves, dead flowers, cardboard (ripped up into small pieces) and other garden waste into the bin.

2. Turn it (mix it) with a spade once a month and it will start to break down. Within a year or two, you'll have a nutrient-rich mulch at the bottom of your compost bin, ready to use on your garden.

1. Or, if you have a bokashi composter, put any food waste into the bin along with some bokashi bran. Once full, keep it sealed for around two weeks to ferment.

2. You can either bury the fermented compost in your borders to add nutrients to your soil or use it to mulch containers or pots with plants.

Planting bulbs for spring

WHY YOU SHOULD GIVE IT A TRY
Putting some time into planting bulbs in autumn is not something you'll regret. When beautiful tulips, daffodils and crocuses pop up in the spring months, you'll be so glad you spent the time in autumn preparing them. The real bonus is that you can't really go wrong with this – so you have no excuse not to give it a go!

WHAT YOU NEED
A selection of pots (one 30cm diameter pot will fit 6–7 bulbs)
Peat-free multipurpose compost
Horticultural grit (optional)

A selection of bulbs – tulips, daffodils and crocuses are my favourites (check the labels before you buy for colour and height)

HOW LONG YOU NEED
15–30 minutes, depending on how many pots you're planting up.

The joy it brings...

—

Knowing that you're planting pops of colour in autumn ready for your enjoyment in spring is a satisfying feeling and you won't regret it!

1. Fill the pots with compost to about three-quarters full. If you want to mix in a little horticultural grit to aid drainage.

2. Place the bulbs into the soil with the hairy bit at the bottom and the little point at the top.

3. Cover the bulbs with more compost, filling the pot to 2cm below the top.

4. Firm down the soil with your fingers, then water and place the pot somewhere sheltered, near the house if you can.

Onions and garlic for next year

WHY YOU SHOULD GIVE IT A TRY
Early to mid-November is usually the best planting time for onions and garlic, so spend a little time outside now and you'll reap the rewards next year – not only will you have homegrown vegetables, but you'll save money at the supermarket, too.

WHAT YOU NEED
Onion sets (immature bulbs) and garlic cloves, which you can buy like bulbs from garden centres or online

Peat-free multipurpose compost

HOW LONG YOU NEED
It takes about 30 minutes to plant a handful of onions and garlic.

The joy it brings...

—

I use both of these vegetables a lot in my cooking, so growing them for myself is really satisfying and the flavours are so much better than shop-bought.

1. Before you plant your onions and garlic, mulch the area where you're going to plant with some peat-free compost (see page 129).

2. Plant the sets and cloves about 2cm deep in the soil, spacing them about 5cm apart.

3. Firm down the soil with your hands.

4. Water well, then wait for your onions and garlic to be ready to enjoy in the summer months.

Lifting dahlias

WHY YOU SHOULD GIVE IT A TRY
This is a money-saving way to enjoy your dahlias again next year. By keeping your dahlia tubers safely stored, they'll last for years.

WHAT YOU NEED
A garden fork (optional)
Cardboard boxes or clean
  plastic plant pots

A cool, dark place to store
  the tubers

HOW LONG YOU NEED
30 minutes.

The joy it brings...

—

This is a gardening ritual that signals the end of autumn. I find it really satisfying knowing that next year they'll be ready to flower again and bring more joy to the garden after hibernating over the winter.

1. Locate the dahlias that have gone over (the colours have faded and the plants are dying back).

2. Wiggle the base of the plant with your hands or garden fork, then lift the dahlia up to reveal the tuber and root system.

3. Brush off the soil from the tuber, give it a wash under the tap and then place it in a clean box or pot.

4. Store in a cool, dark place over autumn and winter (a shed is ideal if you have one), ready to plant again in spring.

Windowsill salad bowl

WHY YOU SHOULD GIVE IT A TRY
Growing salad is quick, easy and cost-effective (not to mention it tastes even better when you pick it fresh). Serving your home-grown salad to your friends and family is an awesome feeling.

WHAT YOU NEED
A pot or selection of pots that will fit on your windowsill

Peat-free multipurpose compost
'Salad bowl' seeds
A pencil

HOW LONG YOU NEED
5–10 minutes.

The joy it brings...

—

There is no greater satisfaction than growing your own salad and saving on the waste and money involved with buying it from the supermarket. It's as fresh as it can be and you'll appreciate every mouthful!

1. Fill the pot with compost to about 3cm from the top and firm down with your fingers. Use a pen to create 2–3cm deep holes in the soil at least 2cm apart.

2. Drop one seed in each hole and then cover over with more compost. Place on a sunny windowsill.

3. Water every day or two, making sure the pot gets plenty of sunlight, and in around 2-3 weeks, you can start cutting off the salad leaves and eating them.

4. If you cut the leaves about 2cm from the base, they will re-grow and you'll have a continuous supply of salad all season.

Autumn flowers perfect for pots

WHY YOU SHOULD GIVE IT A TRY
As the weather gets a little gloomier in the autumn and we lose the summer light and warmth, it's a great little pick-me-up to have colour on your windowsill, on your balcony or dotted around your garden.

WHAT YOU NEED
An attractive pot
Peat-free multipurpose
  compost
Horticultural grit (optional)

Autumn bedding plants, such
  as pansies, violas, cyclamen
  and heathers

HOW LONG YOU NEED
5–10 minutes.

The joy it brings...

—

Planting autumn colour keeps
your garden or outside space bright
and vibrant, boosting your mood
when the weather is grey.

1. Fill the pot with compost to about three-quarters full. If you want to, you can mix in a little horticultural grit to aid drainage.

2. Gently place the colourful bedding plants into the pot. Aim to give each plant a bit of breathing space and don't plant too closely.

3. Add more compost around the plants, filling the pot to about 2cm below the top. Firm down the soil around the plants with your fingers.

4. Water well and place the pot in a place where the bright flowers will catch your eye every morning.

Mulching 101

WHY YOU SHOULD GIVE IT A TRY

Plants get their nutrients from the soil, so it's important to replenish those nutrients by regularly adding a layer of fresh compost or manure. This will keep your garden thriving and looking healthy. Mulching is a little bit like tucking up your plants for the season – it keeps them cosy! It's also a brilliant way to reduce weeds and keep moisture locked into the soil. Mulching is most effective in borders and pots.

WHAT YOU NEED

Peat-free multipurpose compost, farmyard manure or mulch mix (you may need a few bags)

Heavy duty gloves (or a very good hand soap afterwards!)

A fork or rake (optional)

HOW LONG YOU NEED

20–30 minutes.

The joy it brings...

—

The satisfaction of mulching is awesome! It's a perfect activity for a colder day out in the garden and it feels good to be topping up your borders, pots and beds with the nutrients your plants need.

1. Open up your bag of compost and transfer some to a more transportable container , if you have one, for ease.

2. After setting it as close as possible to where you're mulching, empty the compost into your bed, pot or boarder.

3. Using your hands or a spade, gently spread the compost around your plants. You want a nice thick layer of mulch, so don't spread it too thinly.

4. Repeat until all your plants are cosy and nicely tucked in for the colder months ahead.

Win

ter

Colour to get you through winter

WHY YOU SHOULD GIVE IT A TRY
Winter can mean a lack of colour and vitality in the garden, but there are a few flowers that are tough enough to survive the frost. Planting these near your home can really lift your spirits in those colder months.

WHAT YOU NEED
Pots and pot feet (to help excess water drain off on rainy days) or hanging baskets

Peat-free multipurpose compost
Viola and cyclamen plants
Horticultural grit

HOW LONG YOU NEED
15–30 minutes.

The joy it brings...

—

During winter, I love being greeted at the front door by a little colour or glancing out of the window and spotting some unexpected blooms. It gets me through the darker days and reminds me that brighter, spring days are just around the corner.

1. Half-fill the pots or hanging baskets with compost.

2. Carefully position the bedding plants in the pots – they can be quite snug together.

3. Add more compost until the pots are filled to just below the top of the pot, then firm down the soil with your fingers.

4. Water and position the pots on their pot feet or hang the baskets. Add a layer of grit to the top of the pot for decoration and drainage.

Plotting out your vegetable patch

WHY YOU SHOULD GIVE IT A TRY

Growing your own fruit and vegetables is one of the best feelings – tasting that first homegrown crop is something you'll never forget! Taking this on does mean you'll need to be organised, patient and attentive, but as the seasons go by, you'll be so happy you planned ahead and made it happen. However, be careful not to make the mistake I did in my first year of growing – I grew lots of radishes, but later realised that I actually never eat them! So, if you're going to grow your own food, plan and plot in advance so that you can optimise your space and time.

WHAT YOU NEED

Space in the garden or
   for pots on your patio
   or balcony

A measuring tape
A notepad and a pencil

HOW LONG YOU NEED

Enough time to think creatively and reflect.

The joy it brings...

—

Growing your own vegetables is one of the most fulfilling activities. And, being more self-sufficient also means you'll need to buy less weekly at the shops, which is good for the planet and your purse.

1. First, think about what you'd like to grow, based on what you love cooking with and eating.

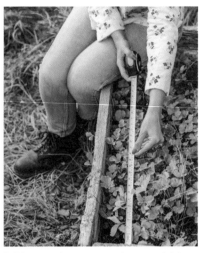

2. Measure the space you have available to you. If you plan to grow in pots, count how many pots you'll use and measure their diameter.

3. Sketch out your space, using these measurements. Consider plant spacing and height (e.g. courgettes need at least 45cm space as they grow outwards, but tomatoes grow upwards so need less).

4. Once you've got a plan, start to work out when you are going to sow your seeds and put together your wishlist! Then you'll be all set for the growing season.

Cutting back

WHY YOU SHOULD GIVE IT A TRY
Preparing your garden for the year ahead is one of the most productive things you can do in the garden in winter. Pruning and cutting back plants keeps things tidy and encourages new, healthy growth in spring. Leaving your cutting back until the end of winter will help wildlife in the winter months by providing them with a habitat.

WHAT YOU NEED
Clean secateurs

HOW LONG YOU NEED
There's no need to do this all at once, so fit it in around your day.

The joy it brings...

—

I find cutting plants back therapeutic and satisfying. It also gives you the chance to get some much-needed fresh air in the winter months.

1. If you have a climbing rose or rose bush, trim back the weaker looking stems or those that have become unruly.

2. If your plant is growing new life at the base, it means you can now remove the old wood from the plant.

3. Where a plant is looking brown or crispy, leave for wildlife and chop back at the end of winter in time for new life to grow in spring.

4. Anything you cut back, chop into small pieces and, if you can, add to your compost.

Planting hyacinths

WHY YOU SHOULD GIVE IT A TRY
Hyacinths are beautiful flowers with a lovely fragrance and they can be grown indoors during winter. When they bloom, they bring such happiness!

WHAT YOU NEED
A pretty pot or container to fit on your windowsill

Peat-free multipurpose compost
Hyacinth bulbs

HOW LONG YOU NEED
5–10 minutes.

The joy it brings...

—

The fragrance of hyacinths is divine and in the gloomy winter months the colour really cheers me up. I hope it brings you some joy, too.

1. Remove your hyacinth bulbs from their existing container by gently squeezing it and slowly prising them out.

2. Half-fill your new container with compost and place the bulbs in upright, with the shoots pointing upwards.

3. Cover over with more compost and firm down the soil with your fingers.

4. Water well, then place on your windowsill and in a few weeks, the hyacinths should flower.

Wildlife-friendly garden hacks

WHY YOU SHOULD GIVE IT A TRY

Creating a wildlife-friendly garden is not only great for the environment, but it adds an extra element of natural beauty to your outdoor space, too. A good place to start is to pop outside every now and again during winter and observe your garden and the wildlife that visits so you can consider how to make your outside space even more welcoming.

WHAT YOU NEED

A birdbath or small water feature (homemade or bought)

Twigs, logs or rocks (find these in your garden or forage them from your local area) or other recycled materials, such as cardboard, old pallets, wood or bricks

A bird box (homemade or bought)

Water, spray bottle and fresh lemon

HOW LONG YOU NEED

The time you need will vary depending on what you choose to make and do.

The joy it brings...

—

Doing your bit for nature and your local wildlife feels undeniably good – and you will enjoy seeing animals, birds and insects thrive thanks to your small but important actions.

1. Water is essential for birds, insects and other wildlife, so a birdbath, small pond or water feature is a great way to provide it.

2. Animals need safe places to hide and rest. Creating a pile of logs, rocks or pallets can provide a habitat for small mammals and insects. Nest boxes and birdhouses can also provide shelter for birds and bats.

3. Food sources, such as berries, seeds and nectar, are important for many species. Consider growing a variety of plants to provide a source of food all year round.

4. Don't use harmful pesticides in your garden, as tempting as it might sometimes feel to see quick progress. Try natural alternatives instead.

Water-saving hacks

WHY YOU SHOULD GIVE IT A TRY
As summers continue to get warmer, collecting rainwater throughout the seasons is worthwhile, both to save on wastage and in case of a hosepipe ban. Rainwater is also better for your garden than water from the tap, which contains limescale. Got a big outside space? Pick a big butt to save as much water as possible.

WHAT YOU NEED
A water butt or a large watertight container that is suitable for outdoors

HOW LONG YOU NEED
About 1 hour.

The joy it brings...

—

When you're recycling what nature gives you, there's no better feeling. Rainwater is free and you can use the water you collect for watering your plants and for other jobs like cleaning your pots (see page 105).

1. If your house or flat allows, choose a downpipe for your water butt and place the water butt stand beneath it. Follow the instructions provided with your water butt to install it, along with the downpipe diverter.

2. Place the lid on top of the water butt and secure it according to the manufacturer's instructions. The lid will help keep debris and insects out of the water, ensuring that it remains clean.

1. If this isn't an option for you, simply place a bucket or tub outside when you're expecting rain. Use the water to fill your watering can and water your plants.

2. Use the water to fill your watering can and water your plants.

Planning for the year ahead

WHY YOU SHOULD GIVE IT A TRY
Taking time to reflect on how things have gone and planning ahead is one of the most important parts of gardening, regardless of the size of your space. In fact, it's all the more important if you have a balcony or small space because planning well means you can maximise the space you have.

WHAT YOU NEED
A notepad and pen or pencil

HOW LONG YOU NEED
1–2 hours.

The joy it brings...

—

Winter can feel long and when it's biting cold I really miss gardening. As soon as the bad weather subsides, I like to get outside and start making plans for spring – it brings me hope and positivity, as I am sure it will for you, too.

1. Reflect on what has been good this year in the garden and what you haven't enjoyed so much.

2. Set goals for you and your garden in the year ahead. What would you like to grow? Is there anything you'd like to change?

3. Sketch out a rough plan on paper or use garden-planning tools available online.

4. Research plants and start to create a shopping list, ready for spring.

Creating a Christmas centrepiece

WHY YOU SHOULD GIVE IT A TRY
Getting outside and hunting for holly, pine cones and mistletoe
is a great way to get into the Christmas spirit, and using what you
find as natural decorations or as part of your festive tablescape
helps us to appreciate nature in all seasons.

WHAT YOU NEED

Secateurs or scissors
A basket to collect
  what you find

A clear glass vase
Fairy lights

HOW LONG YOU NEED
An afternoon or a whole day, if you fancy – you'll just need enough
time to enjoy a lovely wildlife walk and a bit of crafting time.

The joy it brings...

—

The festive period is often
centred around gifts, and I think
it's important to enjoy the gift of
nature at Christmas time, too.

1. Wrap up warm and go on a woodland walk. Collect twigs, pine cones, holly leaves and mistletoe if you are able to, or anything else that catches your eye.

2. When you're home, carefully arrange the items in the vase with some water.

3. Add the fairy lights in and around your foraged items.

4. Place the vase in the centre of your table and enjoy nature at the heart of your Christmas.

Planting out your Christmas tree

WHY YOU SHOULD GIVE IT A TRY
A more sustainable Christmas is better for you and the planet.
If you have the space to reuse a potted tree rather than buying
a cut tree every year, it will save you money. Not only that, your
Christmas tree will be in your garden waiting for its entrance into
the home to signal the start of the festive period. Often, potted
trees are more petite than cut trees, which works well if you have
a small space like I do.

WHAT YOU NEED
A potted Christmas tree
A large, frost-resistant pot
   suitable for outdoor use

Peat-free multipurpose
   compost

HOW LONG YOU NEED
30 minutes.

The joy it brings...

—

Buying and reusing a potted tree
is not only sustainable but joyful – it's
like welcoming an old friend back
into the house!

1. After Christmas, bring your tree outside, and half-fill your large, frost-resistant pot with compost.

2. Gently wiggle your tree out of its existing container, giving the pot a squeeze if it's stubborn to get out.

3. Place your tree into the pot and fill around the base with more compost. The soil should be about 3cm from the top of the pot.

4. Firm down the soil with your hands and place in a sheltered spot until next Christmas, keeping it well watered until then.

A houseplant haven

WHY YOU SHOULD GIVE IT A TRY

If you have limited space outside, then houseplants are a great way to get your gardening fix. Having plants inside the home has also been shown to improve general wellbeing, so what's not to love? The bathroom is the perfect spot for many of the most common houseplants because it's humid. This is a great one to start in the early months of the new year after the excitement of the festive season is over.

WHAT YOU NEED

A selection of houseplants – I suggest a peace lily, cheese plant and snake plant

Decorative pots for each plant

A spray water bottle

HOW LONG YOU NEED

You will only need a little time every week to keep your houseplants happy and thriving.

The joy it brings...

–

I love my weekend routine of looking after my houseplant babies. I water them, tend to them (and yes, maybe I do also speak to them). It's a great way to enjoy gardening in the winter months.

1. Take some time to choose which houseplants you want to invest in, checking the variety and their growing requirements. If your home environment works for them, then go for it.

2. When you get your plants home, water them well. To do this, put the plants in the sink or bath and run cool water through them, then let them drain fully.

3. Place the plants in their decorative pots and position them in a suitable spot where they can thrive.

4. For ongoing care, mist your houseplants with water regularly, as well as watering according to each plant's needs.

What to do when

	J	F	M	A	M	J	J	A	S	O	N	D
Creating a border		🌱	🌱	🌱	🌱							
Sowing pretty cosmos			🌱	🌱								
Planting roses		🌱	🌱	🌱								
A colourful spring display		🌱	🌱	🌱								
Growing your own strawberries			🌱	🌱								
The tomato project		🌱	🌱	🌱								
Setting up plant supports				🌱	🌱							
Chitting and growing potatoes		🌱	🌱									
Growing dahlias				🌱	🌱							
Sweet pea heaven			🌱	🌱								
When and how to water your plants			☀	☀	☀	☀	☀	☀	☀			
Keeping on top of weeds the easy way				☀	☀	☀	☀	☀				

	J	F	M	A	M	J	J	A	S	O	N	D
Tying in your plants				☀	☀	☀	☀	☀	☀			
Deadheading a rose					☀	☀	☀	☀	☀			
Lifting bulbs to store for next year					☀	☀						
Making a water feature in a pot						☀	☀					
Growing herbs on your windowsill					☀	☀	☀					
Summer hanging baskets				☀	☀	☀	☀					
Planting veg						☀	☀	☀				
Jazz up your patio for parties					☀	☀	☀	☀	☀			
Tidying your borders and pots										🍃	🍃	
Cleaning your pots	🍃	🍃	🍃	🍃	🍃	🍃	🍃	🍃	🍃	🍃	🍃	🍃
Making your own bird feeder										🍃	🍃	
Home composting, whatever the size of your garden									🍃	🍃	🍃	
Planting bulbs for spring										🍃	🍃	
Onions and garlic for next year								🍃	🍃	🍃	🍃	

	J	F	M	A	M	J	J	A	S	O	N	D
Lifting dahlias									🍂	🍂	🍂	
Windowsill salad bowl								🍂	🍂	🍂		
Autumn flowers perfect for pots								🍂	🍂	🍂		
Mulching 101								🍂	🍂	🍂	🍂	🍂
Colour to get you through winter	❄										❄	❄
Plotting out your vegetable patch	❄										❄	❄
Cutting back		❄	❄									
Planting hyacinths	❄	❄										
Wildlife-friendly garden hacks	❄	❄										
Water-saving hacks	❄	❄										
Planning for the year ahead	❄	❄	❄									
Creating a Christmas centrepiece												❄
Planting out your Christmas tree	❄											
A houseplant haven	❄	❄	❄									

Gardening notes

<u>Spring</u>

_____

_____

_____

_____

_____

_____

_____

_____

_____

Summer

Autumn

<u>Winter</u>

Helpful terms

ACID SOIL – this usually means soil or potting compost with little or no lime content. When tested it will give a reading of less than pH7.

ALKALINE SOIL – this is usually referred to as 'limy soil'. Alkaline soil contains limestone or chalk and gives a higher reading than pH7 when tested. The soil pH is important because it affects the availability of nutrients in the soil. If your soil is alkaline, you can lower its pH by adding mulch.

ANNUALS – my favourites! These are plants that are grown from seed each year and die after flowering. They have one fabulous year and then they're done!

BEDDING PLANTS – these are wonderful and you'll regularly find them at the garden centre for sale. They're grown and sold when they're just about ready to flower and give a lovely pop of colour in your pots or borders. They're great for hanging baskets too.

BOLTING – this describes when root veg or salad produce flowers before harvesting. It spoils whatever you're growing, so you want to avoid it if you can. Lots of watering in hot weather can prevent bolting.

CLOCHE – I have one of these for the vegetable patch in the garden. A cloche is a plastic or glass cover placed over plants to protect them from frost. Handy for early growing in spring, when the weather is a bit chilly.

CULTIVAR – I don't think I've ever used this word and you probably won't ever need to use it, but if you're ever hanging out with experts, you could always drop it into conversation! A cultivar is the correct name for a variety that's been properly grown and 'cultivated' as opposed to being found in the wild, for example.

DEADHEADING – this is a really satisfying job. It's when you remove dead or faded flowers from plants to encourage growth of new flowers and stop the production of seeds.

DECIDUOUS – this term is used to describe plants that lose their leaves in winter months.

ERICACEOUS PLANTS – these are members of the heather family and include azaleas, camellias and rhododendrons. If you have heavy clay soil like I do, it is not suited to these plants. However, if you have a more acid soil, they are perfect for you!

FERTILISERS – food for plants! Your plants need lovely nutrients to grow, bloom and produce fruits. Certain plants relish certain types of food (a bit like we do, right!?), so it's always good to research what fertiliser your specific plant might like. Generally speaking, tomato food is a really good all rounder, so too is liquid seaweed. Both very much available at your local garden centre.

HARDENING OFF – this is all about preparing your plants for the elements. If you're growing seeds inside or in a greenhouse, your plants will need to steadily be introduced to the outdoors. If you move plants too quickly or they're faced with a big change in temperature, they may go into shock and die. A cold frame is a great place to harden off plants – it's a sort of halfway house between being inside and outside, as it offers protection. A little tip from me if you don't have a cold frame... take your plants outside on a warm and sunny day, and then bring them back in for the evening. Do that over a period of time and then steadily they'll be ready for the world!

HARDY PLANTS – this term is used to refer to plants that can survive frosts so they can be left outside for winter. They're really sturdy!

HERBACEOUS PLANTS – these are plants that lose their leaves in the autumn and grow lovely new ones in the spring.

MULCHING – you'll hear me talk about this a lot! What is it? Well, it's the spreading of a thick layer of goodness to improve your soil, keep down weeds and prevent the soil from drying out too. There are lots of mulches you can use on your soil. Here are some examples: rotted manure, mushroom compost, bark.

PERENNIALS – these are plants that survive for a number of years. Some can be a little short-lived (such as lupins, for example – they're very delicate).

PRICKING OUT – this is a term you need to know if you're growing from seed. It is used to describe moving young seedlings from the trays in which they were grown into larger pots or into the ground. It's a job that requires you to be cautious and gentle!

PRUNING – this describes the cutting back of trees, shrubs and branches to improve flowering and create a much neater shape. Most pruning should be done in cooler weather – so in either spring or autumn. Always prune above a bud or leaf to allow new shoots to sprout from just below where you cut.

WILTING – when your plant looks really sad. You can just tell because its leaves become limp. It might be due to lack of water, or it might be because it's poorly!

Index

Glossary terms are in *italics*

A

acid soil 21, *179*
alkaline soil 21, *179*
allotments 17–18
annuals *179*
aphids 26–7

B

balcony gardens 9, 14, 156
bedding plants *179*
  autumn 126–7
  hanging baskets 87–8
  spring 39–41
  summer 87–8

  winter 138–9
benefits of gardening 6–8, 39
birds 39
  bird feeders 108–9
  pigeons 27
  wildlife friendly gardens 17, 150–1
blackfly 26
bokashi composters 111–12
bolting *179*
borders, creating 30–1
budgeting 15
bulbs
  hyacinths 147–8
  lifting & storing 78–9
  planting 114–15
  tulips 78–9

Acknowledgements

Aside from learning how to be a gardener, writing and developing *Start Growing* has been the most rewarding project I've ever undertaken. But I didn't get here on my own.

The wonderfully warm, kind and brilliant Jason Ingram is behind all of the photography throughout the book. We've had some great moments while shooting this project – from defrosting compost in the depths of the cold winter, to sipping iced coffees in the summer sun. We've really laughed and it's been a tonic at times. Thank you.

Lucie – thank you for giving me the opportunity to write this. I never thought I could. Here we are! We made it.

I will always owe a debt of heartfelt gratitude to Martin Frizell, and a big, heartfelt thank you goes to the whole team who work behind the scenes on *This Morning*. Love to you all.

Emily and Madison and the team at Saatchi, thank you for lifting me up and for everything you have done for me, and continue to do.

Elin – you keep me sane and your love and friendship means more to me than you know.

Dominic – thank you for bringing me back, for calmly reassuring me in the moments when I needed it and most of all, for supporting me.

To Ernie, not only for making the cutest appearances in the book, but for doing so every single day. You bring me joy, no matter the season. My little bub.

My biggest and most grateful thanks go to my family – for always believing in me, banishing my self-doubt and patiently enduring my rollercoaster journey with unconditional love. While the ride is far from over, I hope I've made you proud.

Nanny and Pomp, I hope there are book shops up there so you can have a read. Miss you every single day.

About the author

Daisy Payne is a gardener and TV presenter. After discovering gardening when she bought her first home, Daisy began blogging and creating tutorials on YouTube which got the attention of ITV's *This Morning*. Daisy is now a refreshing rising star in the gardening world, charming viewers with her live seasonal tips and tricks. She's known for bringing a touch of glamour and floral fashion to the gardening world.

Having started gardening just six years ago, she is self-taught and passionate about the joy it brings, and would like to show a more accessible side to the green-fingered world.

Ebury Press, an imprint of Ebury Publishing,
20 Vauxhall Bridge Road,
London SW1V 2SA

Ebury Press is part of the Penguin Random House group of companies
whose addresses can be found at global.penguinrandomhouse.com

Text © Daisy Payne
Photography © Jason Ingram
Design by Studio Polka

First published by Ebury Press in 2024

www.penguin.co.uk

A CIP catalogue record for this book is available from the British Library

ISBN 9781529911718

Colour origination by Altaimage Ltd, London
Printed and bound in Malaysia by Times Offset (M) Sdn Bhd

The authorised representative in the EEA is Penguin Random House
Ireland, Morrison Chambers, 32 Nassau Street, Dublin D02 YH68